'INJUSTICE ANYWHERE IS A THREAT TO JUSTICE EVERYWHERE.'

MARTIN LUTHER KING, JR.
Born 1929, Atlanta, Georgia, USA
Died 1968, Memphis, Tennessee, USA

Written on the margins of a newspaper in an Alabama jail in 1963, Martin Luther King, Jr.'s 'Letter from Birmingham Jail' is a response to eight white Alabama clergymen, who argued that the battle against racial segregation should be fought in the courts – not the streets. 'The Three Dimensions of a Complete Life' was first delivered as a sermon at the New Covenant Baptist Church in Chicago on April 9, 1967. It was later republished in *A Gift of Love* – a collection of Dr Martin Luther King, Jr.'s sermons compiled largely from his book *Strength to Love*.

MARTIN LUTHER KING, JR. IN PENGUIN MODERN CLASSICS
A Gift of Love
Why We Can't Wait

MARTIN LUTHER KING, JR.

Letter from Birmingham Jail

PENGUIN BOOKS

PENGUIN CLASSICS

UK | USA | Canada | Ireland | Australia
India | New Zealand | South Africa

Penguin Books is part of the Penguin Random House group
of companies whose addresses can be found at
global.penguinrandomhouse.com.

Penguin
Random House
UK

This selection first published 2018
001

Set in 11.2/13.75 pt Dante MT Std
Typeset by Jouve (UK), Milton Keynes
Printed in Great Britain by Clays Ltd, St Ives plc

ISBN: 978–0–241–33946–6

www.greenpenguin.co.uk

MIX
Paper from
responsible sources
FSC® C018179

Penguin Random House is committed to a
sustainable future for our business, our readers
and our planet. This book is made from Forest
Stewardship Council® certified paper.

Contents

Letter from Birmingham Jail

April 16, 1963

MY DEAR FELLOW CLERGYMEN:

While confined here in the Birmingham city jail, I came across your recent statement calling my present activities 'unwise and untimely'. Seldom do I pause to answer criticism of my work and ideas. If I sought to answer all the criticisms that cross my desk, my secretaries would have little time for anything other than such correspondence in the course of the day, and I would have no time for constructive work. But since I feel that you are men of genuine good will and that your criticisms are sincerely set forth, I want to try to answer your statement in what I hope will be patient and reasonable terms.

I think I should indicate why I am here in Birmingham, since you have been influenced by the view which argues against 'outsiders coming in'. I have the honor of serving as president of the Southern Christian Leadership Conference, an organization operating in every southern state, with headquarters in Atlanta, Georgia. We have some eighty-five affiliated organizations across the South, and one of them is the Alabama Christian Movement for Human Rights. Frequently we share staff, educational and financial resources with our affiliates. Several months ago the affiliate here in Birmingham asked us to be on call to engage in a nonviolent direct action program if such were deemed necessary. We readily consented, and when the hour came we lived up to our promise. So I, along with several members of my staff, am here because I was invited here. I am here because I have organizational ties here.

But more basically, I am in Birmingham because injustice is here. Just as the prophets of the eighth century B.C. left their villages and carried their 'thus saith the Lord' far beyond the boundaries of their home towns, and just as the Apostle Paul left his village of Tarsus and carried the gospel of Jesus Christ to the far corners of the Greco Roman world, so am I compelled to carry the gospel of freedom beyond my own home town. Like Paul, I must constantly respond to the Macedonian call for aid.

Moreover, I am cognizant of the interrelatedness of all communities and states. I cannot sit idly by in Atlanta and not be concerned about what happens in Birmingham. Injustice anywhere is a threat to justice everywhere.

We are caught in an inescapable network of mutuality, tied in a single garment of destiny. Whatever affects one directly, affects all indirectly. Never again can we afford to live with the narrow, provincial 'outside agitator' idea. Anyone who lives inside the United States can never be considered an outsider anywhere within its bounds.

You deplore the demonstrations taking place in Birmingham. But your statement, I am sorry to say, fails to express a similar concern for the conditions that brought about the demonstrations. I am sure that none of you would want to rest content with the superficial kind of social analysis that deals merely with effects and does not grapple with underlying causes. It is unfortunate that demonstrations are taking place in Birmingham, but it is even more unfortunate that the city's white power structure left the Negro community with no alternative.

In any nonviolent campaign there are four basic steps: collection of the facts to determine whether injustices exist; negotiation; self-purification; and direct action. We have gone through all these steps in Birmingham. There can be no gainsaying the fact that racial injustice engulfs this community. Birmingham is probably the most thoroughly segregated city in the United States. Its ugly record of brutality is widely known. Negroes have experienced grossly unjust treatment in the courts. There have been more unsolved bombings of Negro homes and churches in Birmingham than in any other city in the nation. These are the hard, brutal facts of the case. On the basis of these conditions, Negro leaders sought to negotiate with the city fathers. But the latter consistently refused to engage in good faith negotiation.

Then, last September, came the opportunity to talk with leaders of Birmingham's economic community. In the course of the negotiations, certain promises were made by the merchants – for example, to remove the stores' humiliating racial signs. On the basis of these promises, the Reverend Fred Shuttlesworth and the leaders of the Alabama Christian Movement for Human Rights agreed to a moratorium on all demonstrations. As the weeks and months went by, we realized that we were the victims of a broken promise. A few signs, briefly removed, returned; the others remained. As in so many past experiences, our hopes had been blasted, and the shadow of deep disappointment settled upon us. We had no alternative except to prepare for direct action, whereby we would present our very bodies as a means of laying our case before the conscience of the local and the national community. Mindful of the difficulties involved, we decided to undertake a process of self-purification. We began a series of workshops on nonviolence, and we repeatedly asked ourselves: 'Are you able to accept blows without retaliating?' 'Are you able to endure the ordeal of jail?' We decided to schedule our direct action program for the Easter season, realizing that except for Christmas, this is the main shopping period of the year. Knowing that a strong economic-withdrawal program would be the by-product of direct action, we felt that this would be the best time to bring pressure to bear on the merchants for the needed change.

Then it occurred to us that Birmingham's mayoral election was coming up in March, and we speedily decided to postpone action until after election day. When we discovered that the Commissioner of Public Safety, Eugene 'Bull' Connor, had piled up enough votes to be in the run off, we decided again to postpone action until the day after the run off so that the demonstrations could not be used to cloud the issues. Like many others, we waited to see Mr Connor defeated, and to this end we endured postponement after postponement. Having aided in this community need, we felt that our direct action program could be delayed no longer.

You may well ask: 'Why direct action? Why sit-ins, marches and so forth? Isn't negotiation a better path?' You are quite right in calling for negotiation. Indeed, this is the very purpose of direct action. Nonviolent direct action seeks to create such a crisis and foster such a tension that a community which has constantly refused to negotiate is forced to confront the issue. It seeks so to dramatize the issue that it can no longer be ignored. My citing the creation of tension as part of the work of the nonviolent resister may sound rather shocking. But I must confess that I am not afraid of the word 'tension'. I have earnestly opposed violent tension, but there is a type of constructive, nonviolent tension which is necessary for growth. Just as Socrates felt that it was necessary to create a tension in the mind so that individuals could rise from the bondage of myths and half-truths to the unfettered realm of creative analysis and objective appraisal, so must we see the need for nonviolent gadflies to create the kind of tension in society that will help men rise from the dark depths of prejudice and racism to the majestic heights of understanding and brotherhood. The purpose of our direct action program is to create a situation so crisis-packed that it will inevitably open the door to negotiation. I therefore concur with you in your call for negotiation. Too long has our beloved Southland been bogged down in a tragic effort to live in monologue rather than dialogue.

One of the basic points in your statement is that the action that I and my associates have taken in Birmingham is untimely. Some have asked: 'Why didn't you give the new city administration time to act?' The only answer that I can give to this query is that the new Birmingham administration must be prodded about as much as the outgoing one, before it will act. We are sadly mistaken if we feel that the election of Albert Boutwell as mayor will bring the millennium to Birmingham. While Mr Boutwell is a much more gentle person than Mr Connor, they are both segregationists, dedicated to maintenance of the status quo. I have hope that Mr Boutwell will be reasonable enough to see the futility of massive resistance to desegregation. But he will not see this without pressure from devotees of civil rights. My friends, I must say to you that we have not made a single gain in civil rights without determined legal and nonviolent pressure. Lamentably, it is an historical fact that privileged groups seldom give up their privileges voluntarily. Individuals may see the moral light and voluntarily give up their unjust posture; but, as Reinhold Niebuhr has reminded us, groups tend to be more immoral than individuals.

We know through painful experience that freedom is never voluntarily given by the oppressor; it must be demanded by the oppressed. Frankly, I have yet to engage in a direct action campaign that was 'well timed' in the view of those who have not suffered unduly from the disease of segregation. For years now I have heard the word 'Wait!' It rings in the ear of every Negro with piercing familiarity. This 'Wait' has almost always meant 'Never.' We must come to see, with one of our distinguished jurists, that 'justice too long delayed is justice denied.'

We have waited for more than 340 years for our constitutional and God-given rights. The nations of Asia and Africa are moving with jetlike speed toward gaining political independence, but we still creep at horse and buggy pace toward gaining a cup of coffee at a lunch counter. Perhaps it is easy for those who have never felt the stinging darts of segregation to say, 'Wait.' But when you have seen vicious mobs lynch your mothers and fathers at will and drown your sisters and brothers at whim; when you have seen hate-filled policemen curse, kick and even kill your black brothers and sisters; when you see the vast majority of your twenty million Negro brothers smothering in an airtight cage of poverty in the midst of an affluent society; when you suddenly find your tongue twisted and your speech stammering as you seek to explain to your six-year-old daughter why she can't go to the public amusement park that has just been advertised on television, and see tears welling up in her eyes when she is told that Funtown is closed to colored children, and see ominous clouds of inferiority beginning to form in her little mental sky, and see her beginning to distort her personality by developing an unconscious bitterness toward white people; when you have to concoct an answer for a five-year-old son who is asking: 'Daddy, why do white people treat colored people so mean?'; when you take a cross-county drive and find it necessary to sleep night after night in the uncomfortable corners of your automobile because no motel will accept you; when you are humiliated day in and day out by nagging signs reading 'white' and 'colored'; when your first name becomes 'nigger', your middle name becomes 'boy' (however old you are) and your last name becomes 'John', and your wife and mother are never given the respected title 'Mrs'; when you are harried by day and haunted by night by the fact that you are a Negro, living constantly at tiptoe stance, never quite knowing what to expect next, and are plagued with inner fears and outer resentments; when you are forever fighting a degenerating sense of 'nobodiness'– then you will understand why we find it difficult to wait. There comes a time when the cup of endurance runs over, and men are no longer willing to be plunged into the abyss of despair. I hope, sirs, you can understand our legitimate and unavoidable impatience. You express a great deal of anxiety over our willingness to break laws. This is certainly a legitimate concern. Since we so diligently urge people to obey the Supreme Court's decision of 1954 outlawing segregation in the public schools, at first glance it may seem rather paradoxical for us consciously to break laws. One may well ask: 'How can you advocate breaking some laws and obeying others?' The answer lies in the fact that there are two types of laws: just and unjust. I would be the first to advocate obeying just laws. One has not only a legal but a moral responsibility to obey just laws. Conversely, one has a moral responsibility to disobey unjust laws. I would agree with St Augustine that 'an unjust law is no law at all.'

Now, what is the difference between the two? How does one determine whether a law is just or unjust? A just law is a man-made code that squares with the moral law or the law of God. An unjust law is a code that is out of harmony with the moral law. To put it in the terms of St Thomas Aquinas: an unjust law is a human law that is not rooted in eternal law and natural law. Any law that uplifts human personality is just. Any law that degrades human personality is unjust. All segregation statutes are unjust because segregation distorts the soul and damages the personality. It gives the segregator a false sense of superiority and the segregated a false sense of inferiority. Segregation, to use the terminology of the Jewish philosopher Martin Buber, substitutes an 'I it' relationship for an 'I thou' relationship and ends up relegating persons to the status of things. Hence segregation is not only politically, economically and sociologically unsound, it is morally wrong and sinful. Paul Tillich has said that sin is separation. Is not segregation an existential expression of man's tragic separation, his awful estrangement, his terrible sinfulness? Thus it is that I can urge men to obey the 1954 decision of the Supreme Court, for it is morally right; and I can urge them to disobey segregation ordinances, for they are morally wrong.

Let us consider a more concrete example of just and unjust laws. An unjust law is a code that a numerical or power majority group compels a minority group to obey but does not make binding on itself. This is difference made legal. By the same token, a just law is a code that a majority compels a minority to follow and that it is willing to follow itself. This is sameness made legal. Let me give another explanation. A law is unjust if it is inflicted on a minority that, as a result of being denied the right to vote, had no part in enacting or devising the law. Who can say that the legislature of Alabama which set up that state's segregation laws was democratically elected? Throughout Alabama all sorts of devious methods are used to prevent Negroes from becoming registered voters, and there are some counties in which, even though Negroes constitute a majority of the population, not a single Negro is registered. Can any law enacted under such circumstances be considered democratically structured?

Sometimes a law is just on its face and unjust in its application. For instance, I have been arrested on a charge of parading without a permit. Now, there is nothing wrong in having an ordinance which requires a permit for a parade. But such an ordinance becomes unjust when it is used to maintain segregation and to deny citizens the First Amendment privilege of peaceful assembly and protest.

I hope you are able to see the distinction I am trying to point out. In no sense do I advocate evading or defying the law, as would the rabid segregationist. That would lead to anarchy. One who breaks an unjust law must do so openly, lovingly, and with a willingness to accept the penalty. I submit that an individual who breaks a law that conscience tells him is unjust, and who willingly accepts the penalty of imprisonment in order to arouse the conscience of the community over its injustice, is in reality expressing the highest respect for law.

Of course, there is nothing new about this kind of civil disobedience. It was evidenced sublimely in the refusal of Shadrach, Meshach and Abednego to obey the laws of Nebuchadnezzar, on the ground that a higher moral law was at stake. It was practised superbly by the early Christians, who were willing to face hungry lions and the excruciating pain of chopping blocks rather than submit to certain unjust laws of the Roman Empire. To a degree, academic freedom is a reality today because Socrates practised civil disobedience. In our own nation, the Boston Tea Party represented a massive act of civil disobedience.

We should never forget that everything Adolf Hitler did in Germany was 'legal' and everything the Hungarian freedom fighters did in Hungary was 'illegal'. It was 'illegal' to aid and comfort a Jew in Hitler's Germany. Even so, I am sure that, had I lived in Germany at the time, I would have aided and comforted my Jewish brothers. If today I lived in a Communist country where certain principles dear to the Christian faith are suppressed, I would openly advocate disobeying that country's antireligious laws.

I must make two honest confessions to you, my Christian and Jewish brothers. First, I must confess that over the past few years I have been gravely disappointed with the white moderate. I have almost reached the regrettable conclusion that the Negro's great stumbling block in his stride toward freedom is not the White Citizen's Counciler or the Ku Klux Klanner, but the white moderate, who is more devoted to 'order' than to justice; who prefers a negative peace which is the absence of tension to a positive peace which is the presence of justice; who constantly says: 'I agree with you in the goal you seek, but I cannot agree with your methods of direct action'; who paternalistically believes he can set the timetable for another man's freedom; who lives by a mythical concept of time and who constantly advises the Negro to wait for a 'more convenient season'. Shallow understanding from people of good will is more frustrating than absolute misunderstanding from people of ill will. Lukewarm acceptance is much more bewildering than outright rejection.

I had hoped that the white moderate would understand that law and order exist for the purpose of establishing justice and that when they fail in this purpose they become the dangerously structured dams that block the flow of social progress. I had hoped that the white moderate would understand that the present tension in the South is a necessary phase of the transition from an obnoxious negative peace, in which the Negro passively accepted his unjust plight, to a substantive and positive peace, in which all men will respect the dignity and worth of human personality. Actually, we who engage in nonviolent direct action are not the creators of tension. We merely bring to the surface the hidden tension that is already alive. We bring it out in the open, where it can be seen and dealt with. Like a boil that can never be cured so long as it is covered up but must be opened with all its ugliness to the natural medicines of air and light, injustice must be exposed, with all the tension its exposure creates, to the light of human conscience and the air of national opinion before it can be cured.

In your statement you assert that our actions, even

though peaceful, must be condemned because they precipitate violence. But is this a logical assertion? Isn't this
like condemning a robbed man because his possession
of money precipitated the evil act of robbery? Isn't this
like condemning Socrates because his unswerving commitment to truth and his philosophical inquiries
precipitated the act by the misguided populace in which
they made him drink hemlock? Isn't this like condemning Jesus because his unique God consciousness and
never ceasing devotion to God's will precipitated the evil
act of crucifixion? We must come to see that, as the fed-
eral courts have consistently affirmed, it is wrong to urge
an individual to cease his efforts to gain his basic constitutional rights because the quest may precipitate
violence. Society must protect the robbed and punish
the robber. I had also hoped that the white moderate
would reject the myth concerning time in relation to the
struggle for freedom. I have just received a letter from a
white brother in Texas. He writes: 'All Christians know
that the colored people will receive equal rights eventually, but it is possible that you are in too great a religious
hurry. It has taken Christianity almost two thousand
years to accomplish what it has. The teachings of Christ
take time to come to earth.' Such an attitude stems from
a tragic misconception of time, from the strangely

irrational notion that there is something in the very flow of time that will inevitably cure all ills. Actually, time itself is neutral; it can be used either destructively or constructively. More and more I feel that the people of ill will have used time much more effectively than have the people of good will. We will have to repent in this generation not merely for the hateful words and actions of the bad people but for the appalling silence of the good people. Human progress never rolls in on wheels of inevitability; it comes through the tireless efforts of men willing to be co-workers with God, and without this hard work, time itself becomes an ally of the forces of social stagnation. We must use time creatively, in the knowledge that the time is always ripe to do right. Now is the time to make real the promise of democracy and transform our pending national elegy into a creative psalm of brotherhood. Now is the time to lift our national policy from the quicksand of racial injustice to the solid rock of human dignity.

You speak of our activity in Birmingham as extreme. At first I was rather disappointed that fellow clergymen would see my nonviolent efforts as those of an extremist. I began thinking about the fact that I stand in the middle of two opposing forces in the Negro community. One is a force of complacency, made up in part of Negroes who, as a result of long years of oppression, are so drained of self-respect and a sense of 'somebodiness' that they have adjusted to segregation; and in part of a few middle-class Negroes who, because of a degree of academic and economic security and because in some ways they profit by segregation, have become insensitive to the problems of the masses. The other force is one of bitterness and hatred, and it comes perilously close to advocating violence. It is expressed in the various black nationalist groups that are springing up across the nation, the largest and best known being Elijah Muhammad's Muslim movement. Nourished by the Negro's frustration over the continued existence of racial discrimination, this movement is made up of people who have lost faith in America, who have absolutely repudiated Christianity, and who have concluded that the white man is an incorrigible 'devil'.

I have tried to stand between these two forces, saying that we need emulate neither the 'do nothingism' of the complacent nor the hatred and despair of the black nationalist. For there is the more excellent way of love and nonviolent protest. I am grateful to God that, through the influence of the Negro church, the way of nonviolence became an integral part of our struggle. If this philosophy had not emerged, by now many streets of the South would, I am convinced, be flowing with blood. And I am further convinced that if our white brothers dismiss as 'rabble rousers' and 'outside agitators' those of us who employ nonviolent direct action, and if they refuse to support our nonviolent efforts, millions of Negroes will, out of frustration and despair, seek solace and security in black nationalist ideologies – a development that would inevitably lead to a frightening racial nightmare.

Oppressed people cannot remain oppressed forever. The yearning for freedom eventually manifests itself, and that is what has happened to the American Negro. Something within has reminded him of his birthright of freedom, and something without has reminded him that it can be gained. Consciously or unconsciously, he has been caught up by the Zeitgeist, and with his black brothers of Africa and his brown and yellow brothers of Asia, South America and the Caribbean, the United States Negro is moving with a sense of great urgency toward the promised land of racial justice. If one recognizes this vital urge that has engulfed the Negro community, one should readily understand why public demonstrations are taking place. The Negro has many pent-up resentments and latent frustrations, and he must release them. So let him march; let him make prayer pilgrimages to the city hall; let him go on freedom rides – and try to understand why he must do so. If his repressed emotions are not released in nonviolent ways, they will seek expression through violence; this is not a threat but a fact of history. So I have not said to my people: 'Get rid of your discontent.' Rather, I have tried to say that this normal and healthy discontent can be channeled into the creative outlet of nonviolent direct action. And now this approach is being termed extremist. But though I was initially disappointed at being categorized as an extremist, as I continued to think about the matter I gradually gained a measure of satisfaction from the label. Was not Jesus an extremist for love: 'Love your enemies, bless them that curse you, do good to them that hate you, and pray for them which despitefully use you, and persecute you.' Was not Amos an extremist for justice: 'Let justice roll down like waters and righteousness like an ever flowing stream.' Was not Paul an extremist for the Christian gospel: 'I bear in my body the marks of the Lord Jesus.' Was not Martin Luther an extremist: 'Here I stand; I cannot do otherwise, so help me God.' And John Bunyan: 'I will stay in jail to the end of my days before I make a butchery of my conscience.' And Abraham Lincoln: 'This nation cannot survive half slave and half free.' And Thomas Jefferson: 'We hold these truths to be self-evident, that all men are created equal . . .' So the question is not whether we will be extremists, but what kind of extremists we will be. Will we be extremists for hate or for love? Will we be extremists for the preservation of injustice or for the extension of justice? In that dramatic scene on Calvary's hill three men were crucified. We must never forget that all three were crucified for the same crime – the crime of extremism. Two were extremists for immorality, and thus fell below their environment. The other, Jesus Christ, was an extremist for love, truth and goodness, and thereby rose above his environment. Perhaps the South, the nation and the world are in dire need of creative extremists.

I had hoped that the white moderate would see this need. Perhaps I was too optimistic; perhaps I expected too much. I suppose I should have realized that few members of the oppressor race can understand the deep groans and passionate yearnings of the oppressed race, and still fewer have the vision to see that injustice must be rooted out by strong, persistent and determined action. I am thankful, however, that some of our white brothers in the South have grasped the meaning of this social revolution and committed themselves to it. They are still all too few in quantity, but they are big in quality. Some – such as Ralph McGill, Lillian Smith, Harry Golden, James McBride Dabbs, Ann Braden and Sarah Patton Boyle – have written about our struggle in eloquent and prophetic terms. Others have marched with us down nameless streets of the South. They have languished in filthy, roach-infested jails, suffering the abuse and brutality of policemen who view them as 'dirty nigger-lovers'. Unlike so many of their moderate brothers and sisters, they have recognized the urgency of the moment and sensed the need for powerful 'action' antidotes to combat the disease of segregation. Let me take note of my other major disappointment. I have been so greatly disappointed with the white church and its leadership. Of course, there are some notable exceptions. I am not unmindful of the fact that each of you has taken some significant stands on this issue. I commend you, Reverend Stallings, for your Christian stand on this past Sunday, in welcoming Negroes to your worship service on a nonsegregated basis. I commend the Catholic leaders of this state for integrating Spring Hill College several years ago.

But despite these notable exceptions, I must honestly reiterate that I have been disappointed with the church. I do not say this as one of those negative critics who can always find something wrong with the church. I say this as a minister of the gospel, who loves the church; who was nurtured in its bosom; who has been sustained by its spiritual blessings and who will remain true to it as long as the cord of life shall lengthen.

When I was suddenly catapulted into the leadership of the bus protest in Montgomery, Alabama, a few years ago, I felt we would be supported by the white church.

I felt that the white ministers, priests and rabbis of the South would be among our strongest allies. Instead, some have been outright opponents, refusing to understand the freedom movement and misrepresenting its leaders; all too many others have been more cautious than courageous and have remained silent behind the anaesthetizing security of stained glass windows.

In spite of my shattered dreams, I came to Birmingham with the hope that the white religious leadership of this community would see the justice of our cause and, with deep moral concern, would serve as the channel through which our just grievances could reach the power structure. I had hoped that each of you would understand. But again I have been disappointed.

I have heard numerous southern religious leaders admonish their worshipers to comply with a desegregation decision because it is the law, but I have longed to hear white ministers declare: 'Follow this decree because integration is morally right and because the Negro is your brother.' In the midst of blatant injustices inflicted upon the Negro, I have watched white churchmen stand on the sideline and mouth pious irrelevancies and sanctimonious trivialities. In the midst of a mighty struggle to rid our nation of racial and economic injustice, I have heard many ministers say: 'Those are social issues, with which the gospel has no real concern.' And I have watched many churches commit themselves to a completely other-worldly religion which makes a strange, un-Biblical distinction between body and soul, between the sacred and the secular.

I have traveled the length and breadth of Alabama, Mississippi and all the other southern states. On sweltering summer days and crisp autumn mornings I have looked at the South's beautiful churches with their lofty spires pointing heavenward. I have beheld the impressive outlines of her massive religious education buildings. Over and over I have found myself asking: 'What kind of people worship here? Who is their God? Where were their voices when the lips of Governor Barnett dripped with words of interposition and nullification? Where were they when Governor Wallace gave a clarion call for defiance and hatred? Where were their voices of support when bruised and weary Negro men and women decided to rise from the dark dungeons of complacency to the bright hills of creative protest?'

Yes, these questions are still in my mind. In deep disappointment I have wept over the laxity of the church. But be assured that my tears have been tears of love. There can be no deep disappointment where there is not deep love. Yes, I love the church. How could I do otherwise? I am in the rather unique position of being the son, the grandson and the great-grandson of preachers. Yes, I see the church as the body of Christ. But, oh! How we have blemished and scarred that body through social neglect and through fear of being nonconformists.

There was a time when the church was very powerful – in the time when the early Christians rejoiced at being deemed worthy to suffer for what they believed. In those days the church was not merely a thermometer that recorded the ideas and principles of popular opinion; it was a thermostat that transformed the mores of society. Whenever the early Christians entered a town, the people in power became disturbed and immediately sought to convict the Christians for being 'disturbers of the peace' and 'outside agitators'. But the Christians pressed on, in the conviction that they were 'a colony of heaven', called to obey God rather than man. Small in number, they were big in commitment. They were too God-intoxicated to be 'astronomically intimidated'. By their effort and example they brought an end to such ancient evils as infanticide and gladiatorial contests. Things are different now. So often the contemporary church is a weak, ineffectual voice with an uncertain sound. So often it is an arch-defender of the status quo. Far from being disturbed by the presence of the church, the power structure of the average community is consoled by the church's silent – and often even vocal – sanction of things as they are.

But the judgment of God is upon the church as never before. If today's church does not recapture the sacrificial spirit of the early church, it will lose its authenticity, forfeit the loyalty of millions, and be dismissed as an irrelevant social club with no meaning for the twentieth century. Every day I meet young people whose disappointment with the church has turned into outright disgust.

Perhaps I have once again been too optimistic. Is organized religion too inextricably bound to the status quo to save our nation and the world? Perhaps I must turn my faith to the inner spiritual church, the church within the church, as the true *ekklesia* and the hope of the world. But again I am thankful to God that some noble souls from the ranks of organized religion have broken loose from the paralyzing chains of conformity and joined us as active partners in the struggle for freedom. They have left their secure congregations and walked the streets of Albany, Georgia, with us. They have gone down the highways of the South on tortuous rides for freedom. Yes, they have gone to jail with us. Some have been dismissed from their churches, have lost the support of their bishops and fellow ministers. But they have acted in the faith that right defeated is stronger than evil triumphant. Their witness has been the spiritual salt that has preserved the true meaning of the gospel in these troubled times. They have carved a tunnel of hope through the dark mountain of disappointment. I hope the church as a whole will meet the challenge of this decisive hour. But even if the church does not come to the aid of justice, I have no despair about the future. I have no fear about the outcome of our struggle in Birmingham, even if our motives are at present misunderstood. We will reach the goal of freedom in Birmingham and all over the nation, because the goal of America is freedom. Abused and scorned though we may be, our destiny is tied up with America's destiny. Before the pilgrims landed at Plymouth, we were here. Before the pen of Jefferson etched the majestic words of the Declaration of Independence across the pages of history, we were here. For more than two centuries our forebears labored in this country without wages; they made cotton king; they built the homes of their masters while suffering gross injustice and shameful humiliation – and yet out of a bottomless vitality they continued to thrive and develop. If the inexpressible cruelties of slavery could not stop us, the opposition we now face will surely fail. We will win our freedom because the sacred heritage of our nation and the eternal will of God are embodied in our echoing demands. Before closing I feel impelled to mention one other point in your statement that has troubled me profoundly. You warmly commended the Birmingham police force for keeping 'order' and 'preventing violence'. I doubt that you would have so warmly commended the police force if you had seen its dogs sinking their teeth into unarmed, non-violent Negroes. I doubt that you would so quickly commend the policemen if you were to observe their ugly and inhumane treatment of Negroes here in the city jail; if you were to watch them push and curse old Negro women and young Negro girls; if you were to see them slap and kick old Negro men and young boys; if you were to observe them, as they did on two occasions, refuse to give us food because we wanted to sing our grace together. I cannot join you in your praise of the Birmingham police department.

It is true that the police have exercised a degree of discipline in handling the demonstrators. In this sense they have conducted themselves rather 'nonviolently' in public. But for what purpose? To preserve the evil system of segregation. Over the past few years I have consistently preached that nonviolence demands that the means we use must be as pure as the ends we seek. I have tried to make clear that it is wrong to use immoral means to attain moral ends. But now I must affirm that it is just as wrong, or perhaps even more so, to use moral means to preserve immoral ends. Perhaps Mr Connor and his policemen have been rather nonviolent in public, as was Chief Pritchett in Albany, Georgia, but they have used the moral means of nonviolence to maintain the immoral end of racial injustice. As T. S. Eliot has said: 'The last temptation is the greatest treason: To do the right deed for the wrong reason.'

I wish you had commended the Negro sit-inners and demonstrators of Birmingham for their sublime courage, their willingness to suffer and their amazing discipline in the midst of great provocation. One day the South will recognize its real heroes. They will be the James Merediths, with the noble sense of purpose that enables them to face jeering and hostile mobs, and with the agonizing loneliness that characterizes the life of the pioneer. They will be old, oppressed, battered Negro women, symbolized in a seventy-two-year-old woman in Montgomery, Alabama, who rose up with a sense of dignity and with her people decided not to ride segregated buses, and who responded with ungrammatical profundity to one who inquired about her weariness: 'My feets is tired, but my soul is at rest.' They will be the young high school and college students, the young ministers of the gospel and a host of their elders, courageously and nonviolently sitting-in at lunch counters and willingly going to jail for conscience' sake. One day the South will know that when these disinherited children of God sat down at lunch counters, they were in reality standing up for what is best in the American dream and for the most sacred values in our Judaeo–Christian heritage, thereby bringing our nation back to those great wells of democracy which were dug deep by the founding fathers in their formulation of the Constitution and the Declaration of Independence.

Never before have I written so long a letter. I'm afraid it is much too long to take your precious time. I can assure you that it would have been much shorter if I had been writing from a comfortable desk, but what else can one do when he is alone in a narrow jail cell, other than write long letters, think long thoughts and pray long prayers?

If I have said anything in this letter that overstates the truth and indicates an unreasonable impatience, I beg you to forgive me. If I have said anything that understates the truth and indicates my having a patience that allows me to settle for anything less than brotherhood, I beg God to forgive me.

I hope this letter finds you strong in the faith. I also hope that circumstances will soon make it possible for me to meet each of you, not as an integrationist or a civil rights leader but as a fellow clergyman and a Christian brother. Let us all hope that the dark clouds of racial prejudice will soon pass away and the deep fog of misunderstanding will be lifted from our fear-drenched communities, and in some not too distant tomorrow the radiant stars of love and brotherhood will shine over our great nation with all their scintillating beauty.

Yours for the cause of Peace and Brotherhood,

Martin Luther King, Jr.

The Three Dimensions of a Complete Life

I want to use as the subject from which to preach: 'The Three Dimensions of a Complete Life.' You know, they used to tell us in Hollywood that in order for a movie to be complete, it had to be three-dimensional. Well, this morning I want to seek to get over to each of us that if life itself is to be complete, it must be three-dimensional.

Many, many centuries ago, there was a man by the name of John who found himself in prison out on a lonely, obscure island called Patmos. And I've been in prison just enough to know that it's a lonely experience. And when you are incarcerated in such a situation, you are deprived of almost every freedom, but the freedom to think, the freedom to pray, the freedom to reflect and to meditate. And while John was out on this lonely island in prison, he lifted his vision to high heaven and he saw, descending out of heaven, a new heaven and a new earth. Over in the twenty-first chapter of the book of Revelation, it opens by saying, 'And I saw a new heaven and a new earth. And I John saw the holy city, the new Jerusalem, coming down from God out of heaven.'

And one of the greatest glories of this new city of God that John saw was its completeness. It was not up on one side and down on the other, but it was complete in all three of its dimensions. And so in this same chapter as we looked down to the sixteenth verse, John says, 'The length and the breadth and the height of it are equal.' In other words, this new city of God, this new city of ideal humanity is not an unbalanced entity, but is complete on all sides. Now I think John is saying something here in all of the symbolism of this text and the symbolism of this chapter. He's saying at bottom that life as it should be and life at its best is a life that is complete on all sides.

And there are three dimensions of any complete life to which we can fitly give the words of this text: length, breadth, and height. Now the length of life as we shall use it here is the inward concern for one's own welfare. In other words, it is that inward concern that causes one to push forward, to achieve his own goals and ambitions. The breadth of life as we shall use it here is the outward concern for the welfare of others. And the height of life is the upward reach for God. Now you got to have all three of these to have a complete life.

Now let's turn for the moment to the length of life. I said that this is the dimension of life where we are concerned with developing our inner powers. In a sense this is the selfish dimension of life. There is such a thing as rational and healthy self-interest. A great Jewish rabbi, the late Joshua Leibman, wrote a book some years ago entitled *Peace of Mind*. And he has a chapter in that book entitled 'Love Thyself Properly'. And what he says in that chapter, in substance, is that before you can love other selves adequately, you've got to love your own self properly. You know, a lot of people don't love themselves. And they go through life with deep and haunting emotional conflicts. So the length of life means that you must love yourself.

And you know what loving yourself also means? It means that you've got to accept yourself. So many people are busy trying to be somebody else. God gave all of us something significant. And we must pray every day, asking God to help us to accept ourselves. That means everything. Too many Negroes are ashamed of themselves, ashamed of being black. A Negro got to rise up and say from the bottom of his soul, 'I am somebody. I have a rich, noble, and proud heritage. However exploited and however painful my history has been, I'm black, but I'm black and beautiful.' This is what we've got to say. We've got to accept ourselves. And we must pray, 'Lord, Help me to accept myself every day; help me to accept my tools.'

I remember when I was in college, I majored in sociology, and all sociology majors had to take a course that was required called statistics. And statistics can be very complicated. You've got to have a mathematical mind, a real knowledge of geometry, and you've got to know how to find the mean, the mode, and the median. I never will forget. I took this course and I had a fellow classmate who could just work that stuff out, you know. And he could do his homework in about an hour. We would often go to the lab or the workshop, and he would just work it out in about an hour, and it was over for him. And I was trying to do what he was doing; I was trying to do mine in an hour. And the more I tried to do it in an hour, the more I was flunking out in the course. And I had to come to a very hard conclusion. I had to sit down and say, 'Now, Martin Luther King, Leif Cane has a better mind than you.' Sometimes you have to acknowledge that. And I had to say to myself, 'Now, he may be able to do it in an hour, but it takes me two or three hours to do it.' I was not willing to accept myself. I was not willing to accept my tools and my limitations.

But you know in life we're called upon to do this. A Ford car trying to be a Cadillac is absurd, but if a Ford will accept itself as a Ford, it can do many things that a Cadillac could never do: it can get in parking spaces that a Cadillac can never get in. And in life some of us are

Fords and some of us are Cadillacs. Moses says in 'Green Pastures', 'Lord, I ain't much, but I is all I got.' The principle of self-acceptance is a basic principle in life.

Now the other thing about the length of life: after accepting ourselves and our tools, we must discover what we are called to do. And once we discover it we should set out to do it with all of the strength and all of the power that we have in our systems. And after we've discovered what God called us to do, after we've discovered our life's work, we should set out to do that work so well that the living, the dead, or the unborn couldn't do it any better. Now this does not mean that everybody will do the so-called big, recognized things of life. Very few people will rise to the heights of genius in the arts and the sciences; very few collectively will rise to certain professions. Most of us will have to be content to work in the fields and in the factories and on the streets. But we must see the dignity of all labor.

When I was in Montgomery, Alabama, I went to a shoe shop quite often, known as the Gordon Shoe Shop. And there was a fellow in there that used to shine my shoes, and it was just an experience to witness this fellow shining my shoes. He would get that rag, you know, and he could bring music out of it. And I said to myself, 'This fellow has a PhD in shoe shining.'

What I'm saying to you this morning, my friends,

even if it falls your lot to be a street sweeper, go on out and sweep streets like Michelangelo painted pictures; sweep streets like Handel and Beethoven composed music; sweep streets like Shakespeare wrote poetry; sweep streets so well that all the host of heaven and earth will have to pause and say, 'Here lived a great street sweeper who swept his job well.'

> If you can't be a pine on the top of a hill
> Be a scrub in the valley – but be
> The best little scrub on the side of the hill,
> Be a bush if you can't be a tree.
> If you can't be a highway just be a trail
> If you can't be the sun be a star;
> It isn't by size that you win or fail –
> Be the best of whatever you are.

And when you do this, when you do this, you've mastered the length of life.

This onward push to the end of self-fulfillment is the end of a person's life. Now don't stop here, though. You know, a lot of people get no further in life than the length. They develop their inner powers; they do their jobs well. But do you know, they try to live as if nobody else lives in the world but themselves. And they use everybody as mere tools to get to where they're going. They don't love anybody but themselves. And the only kind of love that they really have for other people is utilitarian love. You know, they just love people that they can use.

A lot of people never get beyond the first dimension of life. They use other people as mere steps by which they can climb to their goals and their ambitions. These people don't work out well in life. They may go for awhile, they may think they're making it all right, but there is a law. They call it the law of gravitation in the physical universe, and it works, it's final, it's inexorable: whatever goes up can come down. You shall reap what you sow. God has structured the universe that way. And he who goes through life not concerned about others will be a subject, a victim of this law.

So I move on and say that it is necessary to add breadth to length. Now the breadth of life is the outward concern for the welfare of others, as I said. And a man has not begun to live until he can rise above the narrow confines of his own individual concerns to the broader concerns of all humanity.

One day Jesus told a parable. You will remember that parable. He had a man that came to him to talk with him about some very profound concerns. And they finally got around to the question, 'Who is my neighbor?' And this man wanted to debate with Jesus. This question could have very easily ended up in thin air as a theological or philosophical debate. But you remember Jesus immediately pulled that question out of thin air and placed it on a dangerous curve between Jerusalem and Jericho. He talked about a certain man who fell among thieves. Two men came by and they just kept going. And then finally another man came, a member of another race, who stopped and helped him. And that parable ends up saying that this good Samaritan was a great man; he was a good man because he was concerned about more than himself.

Now you know, there are many ideas about why the priest and the Levite passed and didn't stop to help that man. A lot of ideas about it. Some say that they were going to a church service, and they were running a little late, you know, and couldn't be late for church, so they kept going because they had to get down to the synagogue. And then there are others who would say that they were involved in the priesthood and consequently there was a priestly law which said that if you were going to administer the sacrament or what have you, you couldn't touch a human body twenty-four hours before worship. Now there's another possibility. It is possible that they were going down to Jericho to organize a Jericho Road Improvement Association. That's another possibility. And they may have passed by because they felt that it was better to deal with the problem from the causal source rather than one individual victim. That's a possibility.

But you know, when I think about this parable, I think of another possibility as I use my imagination. It's possible that these men passed by on the other side because they were afraid. You know, the Jericho Road is a dangerous road. I've been on it and I know. And I never will forget, Mrs King and I were in the Holy Land some time ago. We rented a car and we drove from Jerusalem down to Jericho, a distance of about sixteen miles. You get on that Jericho road – I'm telling you it's a winding, curving, meandering road, very conducive for robbery. And I said to my wife, 'Now I can see why Jesus used this road as the occasion for his parable.' Here you are when you start out in Jerusalem: you are twenty-two hundred feet above sea level, and when you get down to Jericho sixteen miles later – I mean you have sixteen miles from Jerusalem – you're twelve hundred feet below sea level. During the days of Jesus that road came to the point of being known as the 'Bloody Path'. So when I think about the priest and the Levite, I think those brothers were afraid.

They were just like me. I was going out to my father's house in Atlanta the other day. He lives about three or four miles from me, and you go out there by going down Simpson Road. And then when I came back later that night – and brother, I can tell you, Simpson Road is a winding road. And a fellow was standing out there trying to flag me down. And I felt that he needed some help; I knew he needed help. But I didn't know it. I'll be honest with you, I kept going. I wasn't really willing to take the risk.

I say to you this morning that the first question that the priest asked was the first question that I asked on that Jericho Road of Atlanta known as Simpson Road. The first question that the Levite asked was, 'If I stop to help this man, what will happen to me?' But the good Samaritan came by and he reversed the question. Not 'What will happen to me if I stop to help this man?' but 'What will happen to this man if I do not stop to help him?' This was why that man was good and great. He was great because he was willing to take a risk for humanity; he was willing to ask, 'What will happen to this man?' not 'What will happen to me?'

This is what God needs today: men and women who will ask, 'What will happen to humanity if I don't help? What will happen to the civil rights movement if I don't participate? What will happen to my city if I don't vote? What will happen to the sick if I don't visit them?' This is how God judges people in the final analysis.

Oh, there will be a day, the question won't be, 'How many awards did you get in life?' Not that day. It won't be, 'How popular were you in your social setting?' That won't be the question that day. It will not ask how many degrees you've been able to get. The question that day will not be concerned with whether you are a 'PhD' or a 'no D'. It will not be concerned with whether you went to Morehouse or whether you went to 'No House'. The question that day will not be, 'How beautiful is your house?' The question that day will not be, 'How much money did you accumulate? How much did you have in stocks and bonds?' The question that day will not be, 'What kind of automobile did you have?' On that day the question will be, 'What did you do for others?'

Now I can hear somebody saying, 'Lord, I did a lot of things in life. I did my job well; the world honored me for doing my job. I did a lot of things, Lord; I went to school and studied hard. I accumulated a lot of money, Lord; that's what I did.' It seems as if I can hear the Lord of Life saying, 'But I was hungry, and ye fed me not. I was sick, and ye visited me not. I was naked, and ye clothed me not. I was in prison, and you weren't concerned about me. So get out of my face. What did you do for others?' This is the breadth of life.

Somewhere along the way, we must learn that there is nothing greater than to do something for others. And this is the way I've decided to go the rest of my days. That's what I'm concerned about. John, if you and Bernard happen to be around when I come to the latter days and that moment to cross the Jordan, I want you to tell them that I made a request: I don't want a long funeral. In fact, I don't even need a eulogy more than one or two minutes. I hope that I will live so well the rest of the days – I don't know how long I'll live, and I'm not concerned about that – but I hope I can live so well that the preacher can get up and say, 'He was faithful.' That's all, that's enough. That's the sermon I'd like to hear: 'Well done my good and faithful servant. You've been faithful; you've been concerned about others.' That's where I want to go from this point on for the rest of my days. 'He who is greatest among you shall be your servant.' I want to be a servant. I want to be a witness for my Lord, to do something for others.

And don't forget in doing something for others that you have what you have because of others. Don't forget that. We are tied together in life and in the world. And you may think you got all you got by yourself. But you know, before you got out here to church this morning, you were dependent on more than half of the world. You get up in the morning and go to the bathroom, and you reach over for a bar of soap, and that's handed to you by a Frenchman. You reach over for a sponge, and that's given to you by a Turk. You reach over for a towel, and that comes to your hand from the hands of a Pacific Islander. And then you go on to the kitchen to get your breakfast. You reach on over to get a little coffee, and that's poured in your cup by a South American. Or maybe you decide that you want a little tea this morning, only to discover that that's poured in your cup by a Chinese. Or maybe you want a little cocoa, that's poured in your cup by a West African. Then you want a little bread and you reach over to get it, and that's given to you by the hands of an English-speaking farmer, not to mention the baker. Before you get through eating breakfast in the morning, you're dependent on more than half the world. That's the way God structured it; that's the way God structured this world. So let us be concerned about others because we are dependent on others.

But don't stop here either. You know, a lot of people master the length of life, and they master the breadth of life, but they stop right there. Now if life is to be complete, we must move beyond our self-interest. We must move beyond humanity and reach up, way up for the God of the universe, whose purpose changeth not.

Now a lot of people have neglected this third dimension. And you know, the interesting thing is a lot of people neglect it and don't even know they are neglecting it. They just get involved in other things. And you know, there are two kinds of atheism. Atheism is the theory that there is no God. Now one kind is a theoretical kind, where somebody just sits down and starts thinking about it, and they come to a conclusion that there is no God. The other kind is a practical atheism, and that kind goes out of living as if there is no God. And you know there are a lot of people who affirm the existence of God with their lips, and they deny his existence with their lives. You've seen these people who have a high blood pressure of creeds and an anemia of deeds. They deny the existence of God with their lives and they just become so involved in other things. They become so involved in getting a big bank account. They become so involved in getting a beautiful house, which we all should have. They become so involved in getting a beautiful car that they unconsciously just forget about God. There are those who become so involved in looking at the man-made lights of the city that they unconsciously forget to rise up and look at that great cosmic light and think about it – that gets up in the eastern horizon every morning and moves across the sky with a kind of symphony of motion and paints its technicolor across the blue – a light that man can never make. They become so involved in looking at the skyscraping buildings of the Loop of Chicago or Empire State Building of New York that they unconsciously forget to think about the gigantic mountains that kiss the skies as if to bathe their peaks in the lofty blue – something that man could never make. They become so busy thinking about radar and their television that they unconsciously forget to think about the stars that bedeck the heavens like swinging lanterns of eternity, those stars that appear to be shiny, silvery pins sticking in the magnificent blue pincushion. They become so involved in thinking about man's progress that they forget to think about the need for God's power in history. They end up going days and days not knowing that God is not with them.

And I'm here to tell you today that we need God. Modern man may know a great deal, but his knowledge does not eliminate God. And I tell you this morning that God is here to stay. A few theologians are trying to say that God is dead. And I've been asking them about it because it disturbs me to know that God died and I didn't have a chance to attend the funeral. They haven't been able to tell me yet the date of his death. They haven't been able to tell me yet who the coroner was that pronounced him dead. They haven't been able to tell me yet where he's buried.

You see, when I think about God, I know his name. He said somewhere, back in the Old Testament, 'I want you to go out, Moses, and tell them "I Am" sent you.' He said just to make it clear, let them know that 'my last name is the same as my first, "I Am that I Am." Make that clear. I Am.' And God is the only being in the universe that can say 'I Am' and put a period behind it. Each of us sitting here has to say, 'I am because of my parents; I am because of certain environmental conditions; I am because of certain hereditary circumstances; I am because of God.' But God is the only being that can just say, 'I Am' and stop right there. 'I Am that I Am.' And He's here to stay. Let nobody make us feel that we don't need God.

As I come to my conclusion this morning, I want to say that we should search for him. We were made for God, and we will be restless until we find rest in him. And I say to you this morning that this is the personal faith that has kept me going. I'm not worried about the future. You know, even on this race question, I'm not worried. I was down in Alabama the other day, and I started thinking about the state of Alabama where we worked so hard and may continue to elect the Wallaces. And down in my home state of Georgia, we have another sick governor by the name of Lester Maddox. And all of these things can get you confused, but they don't worry me. Because the God that I worship is a God that has a way of saying even to kings and even to governors, 'Be still, and know that I am God.' And God has not yet turned over this universe to Lester Maddox and Lurleen Wallace. Somewhere I read, 'The earth is the Lord's and the fulness thereof,' and I'm going on because I have faith in Him. I do not know what the future holds, but I do know who holds the future. And if He'll guide us and hold our hand, we'll go on in.

I remember down in Montgomery, Alabama, an experience that I'd like to share with you. When we were in the midst of the bus boycott, we had a marvelous old lady that we affectionately called Sister Pollard. She was a wonderful lady about seventy-two years old and she was still working at that age. During the boycott she would walk every day to and from work. She was one that somebody stopped one day and said, 'Wouldn't you like to ride?' And she said, 'No.' And then the driver moved on and stopped and thought, and backed up a little and said, 'Well, aren't you tired?' She said, 'Yes, my feets is tired, but my soul is rested.'

She was a marvelous lady. And one week I can remember that I had gone through a very difficult week. Threatening calls had come in all day and all night the night before, and I was beginning to falter and to get weak within and to lose my courage. And I never will forget that I went to the mass meeting that Monday night very discouraged and a little afraid, and wondering whether we were going to win the struggle. And I got up to make my talk that night, but it didn't come out with strength and power. Sister Pollard came up to me after the meeting and said, 'Son, what's wrong with you?' Said, 'You didn't talk strong enough tonight.'

And I said, 'Nothing is wrong, Sister Pollard, I'm all right.'

She said, 'You can't fool me.' Said, 'Something wrong with you.' And then she went on to say these words, 'Is the white folks doing something to you that you don't like?'

I said, 'Everything is going to be all right, Sister Pollard.'

And then she finally said, 'Now come close to me and let me tell you something one more time, and I want you to hear it this time.' She said, 'Now I done told you we is with you.' She said, 'Now, even if we ain't with you, the Lord is with you.' And she concluded by saying, 'The Lord's going to take care of you.'

And I've seen many things since that day. I've gone through many experiences since that night in Montgomery, Alabama. Since that time Sister Pollard has died. Since that time I've been in more than eighteen jail cells. Since that time I've come perilously close to death at the hands of a demented Negro woman. Since that time I've seen my home bombed three times. Since that time I've had to live every day under the threat of death. Since that time I've had many frustrating and bewildering nights. But over and over again I can still hear Sister Pollard's words: 'God's going to take care of you.' So today I can face any man and any woman with my feet solidly placed on the ground and my head in the air because I know that when you are right, God will fight your battle.

> Darker yet may be the night,
> Harder yet may be the fight.
> Just stand up for that which is right.

It seems that I can hear a voice speaking even this morning, saying to all of us, 'Stand up for what is right. Stand up for what is just. Lo, I will be with you even until the end of the world.' Yes, I've seen the lightning flash. I've heard the thunder roll. I've felt sin-breakers dashing, trying to conquer my soul. But I heard the voice of Jesus saying still to fight on. He promised never to leave me, never to leave me alone. No, never alone. No, never alone. He promised never to leave me, never to leave me alone. And I go on in believing that. Reach out and find the breadth of life.

You may not be able to define God in philosophical terms. Men through the ages have tried to talk about him. Plato said that he was the Architectonic Good. Aristotle called him the Unmoved Mover. Hegel called him the Absolute Whole. Then there was a man named Paul Tillich who called him Being-Itself. We don't need to know all of these high-sounding terms. Maybe we have to know him and discover him another way. One day you ought to rise up and say, 'I know him because he's a lily of the valley. He's a bright and morning star. He's a rose of Sharon. He's a battle-axe in the time of Babylon.' And then somewhere you ought to just reach out and say, 'He's my everything. He's my mother and my father. He's my sister and my brother. He's a friend to the friendless.' This is the God of the universe. And if you believe in him and worship him, something will happen in your life. You will smile when others around you are crying. This is the power of God.

Go out this morning. Love yourself, and that means rational and healthy self-interest. You are commanded to do that. That's the length of life. Then follow that: Love your neighbor as you love yourself. You are commanded to do that. That's the breadth of life. And I'm going to take my seat now by letting you know that there's a first and even greater commandment: 'Love the Lord thy God with all thy heart, with all thy soul, with all thy strength.' I think the psychologist would just say with all thy personality. And when you do that, you've got the breadth of life.

And when you get all three of these together, you can walk and never get weary. You can look up and see the morning stars singing together, and the sons of God shouting for joy. When you get all of these working together in your very life, judgement will roll down like waters, and righteousness like a mighty stream.

When you get all the three of these together, the lamb will lie down with the lion.

When you get all three of these together, you look up and every valley will be exalted, and every hill and mountain will be made low; the rough places will be made plain, and the crooked places straight; and the glory of the Lord shall be revealed and all flesh will see it together.

When you get all three of these working together, you will do unto others as you'd have them do unto you.

When you get all three of these together, you will recognize that out of one blood God made all men to dwell upon the face of the earth . . .*

---

* Recording interrupted.